IT'S TIME TO EAT CHIPS AND QUESO

It's Time to Eat CHIPS AND QUESO

Walter the Educator

Silent King Books
A WhichHead Entertainment Imprint

Copyright © 2024 by Walter the Educator

All rights reserved. No part of this book may be reproduced in any manner whatsoever without written per- mission except in the case of brief quotations embodied in critical articles and reviews.

First Printing, 2024

Disclaimer

This book is a literary work; the story is not about specific persons, locations, situations, and/or circumstances unless mentioned in a historical context. Any resemblance to real persons, locations, situations, and/or circumstances is coincidental. This book is for entertainment and informational purposes only. The author and publisher offer this information without warranties expressed or implied. No matter the grounds, neither the author nor the publisher will be accountable for any losses, injuries, or other damages caused by the reader's use of this book. The use of this book acknowledges an understanding and acceptance of this disclaimer.

It's Time to Eat CHIPS AND QUESO is a collectible early learning book by Walter the Educator suitable for all ages belonging to Walter the Educator's Time to Eat Book Series. Collect more books at WaltertheEducator.com

USE THE EXTRA SPACE TO TAKE NOTES AND DOCUMENT YOUR MEMORIES

CHIPS AND QUESO

Chips and queso, warm and bright,

It's Time to Eat Chips and Queso

A tasty treat, a snack delight!

Crunchy chips, cheese so gooey,

It's snack time fun, all warm and chewy.

The queso's golden, smooth, and hot,

A creamy dip we love a lot!

We dip a chip and take a bite,

Chips and queso feel just right.

Some like it plain, some with spice,

Queso is yummy, queso is nice!

With every scoop, so soft and warm,

Chips and queso are our charm.

The chips go crunch, the queso flows,

Each bite is fun from head to toes!

With every dip, with every taste,

Chips and queso never waste.

It's Time to Eat

Chips

and

Queso

Yellow and melty, thick and smooth,

Chips and queso set the mood.

Snack time fun with cheese galore,

Chips and queso, we want more!

Sometimes with peppers, spicy and green,

Or just with cheese, it's a snack supreme.

Dip and munch, and dip again,

Chips and queso are our friends.

At a party or with lunch,

Chips and queso, crunch by crunch.

A little bowl of cheesy cheer,

Chips and queso, snack time's here!

We gather around, we dip and grin,

Chips and queso, let's dig in!

It's Time to Eat Chips and Queso

Each little bite is soft and bold,

Chips and queso never get old.

So grab a chip, don't let it drip,

Take a scoop, a yummy dip!

Queso warm, and chips so neat,

Together they're the perfect treat.

Cheese so melty, chips so crisp,

Chips and queso are pure bliss.

A snack so fun, so gooey and great,

It's Time to Eat

Chips and Queso

Chips and queso, time to celebrate!

ABOUT THE CREATOR

Walter the Educator is one of the pseudonyms for Walter Anderson. Formally educated in Chemistry, Business, and Education, he is an educator, an author, a diverse entrepreneur, and he is the son of a disabled war veteran. "Walter the Educator" shares his time between educating and creating. He holds interests and owns several creative projects that entertain, enlighten, enhance, and educate, hoping to inspire and motivate you. Follow, find new works, and stay up to date with Walter the Educator™

at WaltertheEducator.com

Milton Keynes UK
Ingram Content Group UK Ltd.
UKHW020047271124
451585UK00012B/1106